INTERPRETATION OF ACCOUNTS

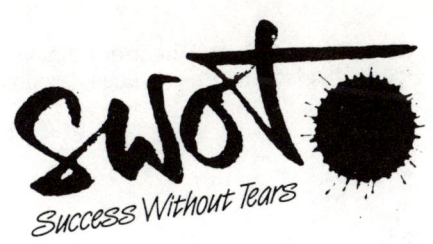

INTERPRETATION OF ACCOUNTS

NEIL D. STEIN FCA, ATII.

First published in Great Britain 1986 by Financial Training Publications Limited, Avenue House, 131 Holland Park Avenue, London W11 4UT

© Neil D. Stein, 1986

ISBN: 1 85185 035 X

Typeset by LKM Typesetting Ltd, London EC1
Printed by Burgess Ltd, Abingdon

All rights reserved. No part of this book may be reproduced or transmitted in any form or by any means, electronic or mechanical, including photocopying, recording, or any information storage or retrieval system without prior permission from the publisher.

CONTENTS

1	Introduction	1
2	Why interpretation?	3
3	Basic techniques	4
4	Report writing	24
5	A basic example	26
6	A more advanced example	31
7	Test question and answer	42

About the author

After periods in the profession and in industry, Neil Stein has been involved in accountancy education since 1965, lecturing in both the public and the private sectors.

He has written a number of study manuals and books on accountancy, auditing and taxation for all levels of the professional accountancy examinations, and is a regular contributor to the Certified Accountants Students' Newsletter.

He is currently senior lecturer in accountancy at Ealing College of Higher Education.

1 INTRODUCTION

Questions on interpreting financial statements can appear in literally *all* the financial accounting papers in the professional examinations. The objectives of this book are to provide:

(a) an introduction to interpretation for students at the earlier examination levels;
(b) a revision and reminder of technique for those at a more advanced level;
(c) guidelines for report writing.

It will help students of the following examinations:

Professional body	Introduction	Revision
Chartered Association of Certified Accountants (ACCA)	Level 1 Accounting	Level 2 Advanced Accounting Practice Level 3 Advanced Financial Accounting
Institute of Chartered Accountants in England and Wales (ICAEW)	Foundation Accounting (existing and new syllabus) (or exempting examinations)	PEII Financial Accounting II New syllabus: PEII Financial Accounting I and Financial Accounting 2
Institute of Chartered Accountants of Scotland (ICAS)	Part II Examination: Interpretation of Financial Information — External Reporting	
Institute of Chartered Accountants in Ireland (ICAI)	Financial Accounting I Financial Accounting II	Financial Accounting III

Professional body	Introduction	Revision
Institute of Cost and Management Accountants (ICMA)	1986: Financial Accounting 2 1987 onwards: Stage 2: Financial Accounting	Financial Accounting 3 Financial Management Stage 3: Advanced Financial Accounting Stage 4: All papers
Association of International Accountants (AIA)	Financial Accounting I Financial Accounting II	Financial Accounting III
Institute of Chartered Secretaries and Administrators (ICSA)	Introduction to Accounting	Financial Accounting
Society of Company and Commercial Accountants (SCCA)	Part 1 Accounting Part 3 Financial Accounting	Part 4 Financial Management
Association of Accounting Technicians (AAT)	Paper 5 Accounting Paper 9 Financial Accounting	
Institute of Bankers (IOB)	Bankers' Conversion Course: Structure of Accounts Stage 2: Accountancy	

This book will also be found useful for any other examination in which interpretation of accounts appears.

2 WHY INTERPRETATION?

Although financial statements have to be prepared by law for most companies they are only of real value if useful information can be obtained from them. Having prepared the financial statements it is necessary to study them to draw conclusions from them about a company's affairs.

Such analysis is of obvious concern and value to the company's own management. In addition, *The Corporate Report* listed the external users of financial statements as:

(a) existing and potential future shareholders;
(b) loan creditors;
(c) employees;
(d) financial analysts and advisers;
(e) business contacts — these include customers and suppliers and, in a different sense, competitors, business rivals and those interested in mergers, amalgamations and takeovers;
(f) the government, including tax authorities;
(g) the general public, including consumer and environmental groups.

These users have a variety of information needs, and the importance they will attach to different areas will also vary. There are some basic areas in which most users will be interested:

(a) profitability;
(b) solvency;
(c) management efficiency;
(d) gearing.

We may identify other areas which will be of special concern to particular user groups:

(e) return for investors;
(f) employment statistics.

3 BASIC TECHNIQUES

The users listed in section 2 above are all interested in *comparing* information about the company under review — comparing it with other companies, comparing current results with the past or with budgets.

To facilitate comparison, information for interpretation is normally presented in the form of percentages or ratios, so that the actual size of the figures does not obscure comparison. This means that details for two companies of completely different size can still be meaningfully compared.

So what are the relevant percentages and ratios? Let us take each of the headings we identified in section 2 and see what ratios help us to compare and understand them, using an illustrative profit and loss account and balance sheet to provide figures.

Auburn Ltd: Balance sheet as at 31 March 19X5

	Cost £000	Aggregate depreciation £000	Net book value £000
Tangible fixed assets	5,000	2,000	3,000
Current assets:			
Stock			
Raw materials	1,000		
Work-in-progress	400		
Finished goods	800		
		2,200	
Debtors		1,300	
Cash		300	
Carried forward		3,800	3,000

	£000	£000
Brought forward	3,800	3,000
Less:		
Creditors — amounts falling due within one year (including dividend £200,000 and taxation £315,000)	1,800	2,000
		5,000
Less:		
Creditors — amounts falling due after more than one year: 12% Debentures		2,000
		3,000
Share capital and reserves:		
Ordinary share capital: 2,000,000 £1 shares		2,000
Profit and loss account		1,000
		3,000

Auburn Ltd: Profit and loss account for the year ended 31 March 19X5

	£000	£000
Sales (all on credit)		9,000
Less: Cost of sales		
Materials	3,500	
Labour	2,000	
Sundries	500	
		6,000
Gross profit carried forward		3,000

	£000
Brought forward	3,000
Less: Expenses, including interest on debentures £240,000	2,100
Net profit	900
Less: Taxation (35%)	315
	585
Less: Proposed ordinary dividend	200
	385
Unappropriated profit brought forward	615
	1,000

3.1 Profitability

Profitability can be measured by reference to sales or by reference to capital employed.

The three main ratios we consider are:

(a) *gross* profit as a percentage of *sales*;

(b) *net* trading profit (normally net of all expenses but not net of tax) as a percentage of *sales*;

(c) net profit (before interest and tax, or after tax) as a percentage of *capital employed*.

The first two of these are fairly straightforward, the third a little more complicated.

Gross profit as a percentage of sales

Gross profit is sales revenue less the cost of goods sold. All or nearly all the costs charged in the calculation will be *variable costs* — that is, costs which vary in acordance with production or sales.

In a wholesaling or retailing business we might therefore expect the gross profit as a percentage of sales to remain steady, *as long as the business is able to pass on the effect of any price increases.*

It follows that any major deviation in the percentage needs urgent investigation, as it may indicate error or fraud in one of more of the trading account items. This is indeed the main use of the gross profit percentage, and is important for all users with a special interest in errors or fraud — the company's management, auditors and inspectors of taxes.

It also tells us something about the company's pricing policy. A high gross profit percentage implies that the operation may be based on charging high prices and thus achieving a low sales volume. Alternatively, a low gross profit percentage may mean that prices are being reduced to the minimum to achieve high sales volume.

In a manufacturing business the gross profit percentage is liable to fluctuate more, because actual costs of production are likely to vary. Nevertheless, it is worth calculating the ratio, and variations in it should still be investigated, and in this respect it is important to verify, if possible, how manufacturing overhead has been treated.

For Auburn Ltd the gross profit as a percentage of sales is:

$$3,000/9,000 \times 100 = 33\tfrac{1}{3}\%$$

On its own, this information is of very little value. We need to *compare* the 33⅓% with:

(a) the corresponding figure for previous periods;
(b) the budgeted figure for this period;
(c) figures for other companies in the same industry.

Question

Try this question about gross profit percentages: How will the following events affect the gross profit percentage of a business?

(a) an increase in sales volume;

(b) an increase in selling price, not accompanied by any increase in costs;

(c) an increase in costs of £1 per unit purchased, passed on to customers by increasing selling price by £1 per unit;

(d) the sale of some slow-moving items at less than normal price;

(e) theft of stock by staff or customers;

(f) theft of cash from proceeds of cash sales;

(g) an unusually high level of bad debts;

(h) an error in the cut-off procedure at the year end.

Answer

(a) No automatic effect, if the unit cost of sales and sale prices remain as before.

(b) GP percentage will increase.

(c) GP percentage will go down, because no profit is being taken on the price increase.

(d) GP percentage will go down.

(e) Overall GP percentage will go down.

(f) Overall GP percentage will go down.

(g) GP percentage is unaffected, as the cost of bad debts is charged in the profit and loss account and will not affect the trading account items.

(h) GP percentage will be affected up or down depending on the direction of the error and the items affected.

Net trading profit (before interest and tax) as a percentage of sales

We take the *trading* profit so that the result is not distorted by the inclusion of non-trading income like rents or interest received and by interest payable.

The figure for Auburn Ltd is:

$(900 + 240)/9,000 \times 100 = 12.67\%$

The value of the ratio is that it measures the company's success in earning profit from its operations. As with the gross profit percentage, the figure for one company for one year is of little value. We need the corresponding percentages for earlier years, or data for other similar companies.

One limitation on the use of the ratio is that the percentage is likely to rise as turnover rises, because most of the expenses in the profit and loss account are fixed, and a rising turnover should mean that a larger gross profit is available to meet these fixed expenses. If net profit does not rise when turnover rises, this could mean that the gross profit margin is being cut to achieve higher sales (a movement in the gross profit percentage will confirm this), or perhaps higher expenditure has been made on advertising and other selling costs which has increased sales (analysis and comparison of individual expense headings in the profit and loss account will confirm this).

Net profit as a percentage of capital employed

This is also called *return on capital employed* (ROCE). It sounds like *the* ratio to tell us about a company's performance. So it is, but its calculation is not as simple as it might seem at first sight. There are many ways of calculating it, some correct and some not. Let us examine some of the alternatives.

Net profit   We could take net profit before or after tax, and in each case before or after interest. Non-trading items could be included or excluded.

Capital employed This could be equity (ordinary shareholders') capital or equity capital plus preference shares and loan capital. Bank overdraft could also be regarded as part of capital employed. Capital employed could also be defined in terms of assets, as fixed assets plus net current assets. Goodwill could be included or excluded.

So how do we find a way through this maze of alternatives? The important thing is that the profit measure chosen must be consistent with the capital measure chosen.

Let us examine the point about consistency by using figures from Auburn Ltd.

	Capital employed £000
Shareholders' capital	3,000
Loan capital	2,000
Total capital (= fixed assets plus net current assets)	5,000

What profit (pre-tax) has been earned by the use of the £5,000,000 total capital? The net profit is £900,000, but this is after charging interest. We need the profit *before* interest if we want the profit generated by the use of the total capital. In other words we must use the figure of £1,140,000 we used in calculating the net profit as a percentage of sales. We may tabulate the figures as follows:

	Capital employed £000		Pre-tax profit £000
Shareholders' capital	3,000	→	900
Loan capital	2,000	→	240
Total capital	5,000	→	1,140

The total profit is £1,140,000. £240,000 of this has been paid out as debenture interest, leaving £900,000 as the return for shareholders. If the bank overdraft is regarded as a part of capital employed, the interest on it must also be added back. Only the shareholders' capital of £3,000,000 will relate to the post-tax profit of £585,000 as this is entirely attributable to them.

3.2 Liquidity and financial soundness

Two main ratios measure a company's ability to pay its debts:

(a) The current ratio (also known as the working capital ratio):

$$\frac{\text{Current assets}}{\text{Current liabilities}} : 1$$

(b) The quick ratio (also known as the liquid ratio or the acid test):

$$\frac{\text{Quick assets*}}{\text{Current liabilities}} : 1$$

*Quick assets are current assets which can be realised into cash within the time allowed for payment of the current liabilities. Quick assets are normally taken to be current assets other than stock.

An alternative form of the quick ratio is to take:

$$\frac{\text{Quick assets}}{\text{Quick liabilities}} : 1$$

The second form of the ratio is probably a better indicator of a company's true ability to meet its obligations as they fall due, but the analysis of creditors necessary for its calculation is often not available, either in practice or in examination questions.

For Auburn Ltd the ratios are:

Current ratio $\quad \dfrac{3{,}800}{2{,}000} : 1 = 1.9{:}1$

Quick ratio $\quad \dfrac{1{,}600}{2{,}000} : 1 = 0.8{:}1$

If tax were excluded from the current liabilities in an attempt to arrive at quick liabilities we should have:

$$\dfrac{1{,}600}{1{,}350} : 1 = 1.19{:}1$$

It is reasonable to do this in the present example, because the accounting date is 31 March and thus the due date for payment of tax is 1 January — nine months later. If the accounting date is 30 April to 31 December, it is possible that two years' tax liabilities are included in the balance sheet and that one of these is due almost immediately.

Note that these ratios are conventionally expressed with '1' as the right-hand side of the ratio. This is to facilitate comparison.

In considering how to interpret the liquidity ratios, let us begin with the second form of the quick ratio — quick assets divided by quick liabilities. If this is less than 1:1, then surely the company is going to have trouble in paying its creditors as they fall due, unless it has an unused bank overdraft facility.

The other ratios, however, vary greatly from industry to industry. An efficient retailer, for example, may well have a *current ratio* of little more than 1:1, and a liquid ratio when all current liabilities are considered of much less than 1:1, perhaps 0.5:1. An average manufacturing company might have a current ratio of around 1.5:1.

It should not be thought that the higher the ratio the more secure the company is. An excessively high ratio may mean that too much of the company's resources is tied up in stocks, debtors and cash balances, the first two of which are not producing profit and the last of which is not being effectively employed in the business if the amount is excessive. Management's overall objective in this area should be to maintain the ratios at the lowest level consistent with paying creditors in such a way as to maintain or improve the company's credit status.

One problem in interpreting liquidity ratios is the treatment of bank overdraft. Though technically a current liability, and in fact theoretically liable to be repaid on demand, many companies use bank overdrafts as semi-permanent sources of finance. If that is indeed the status of the overdraft, it is probably best to exclude it from the calculations.

Yet again, the value of the ratio is the trend of values over several years. If the company is already operating efficiently, the ratios are likely to remain fairly steady, and a sudden drop may well indicate liquidity problems if there is no special factor affecting them.

3.3 Management efficiency

Ratios in this area attempt to appraise the efficiency of management in various areas. The first three ratios considered tell us something about the management's efficiency in controlling the main elements of working capital — stock, debtors and creditors. Thus they help in the interpretation of the liquidity ratios dealt with in the previous paragraph.

Overall stock turnover

This is the ratio between cost of sales and average *total* stock, including raw materials, work-in-progress and finished goods. It gives a general indication of the efficiency of management in controlling stock levels. It is either:

$$\frac{\text{Cost of sales}}{\text{Average total stock}} = \text{No. of times stock is turned over in the year}$$

or:

$$\frac{\text{Average total stock}}{\text{Cost of sales}} \times 365 = \text{No. of days' sales represented by stock}$$

Figures for Auburn Ltd are:

$$\frac{6,000}{2,200} = 2.7 \text{ times} \quad and \quad \frac{2,200}{6,000} \times 365 = 134 \text{ days}$$

A more precise picture of the position is given by the ratios below, which deal with the elements of total stock. The average stock is used in these formulas, but for examination purposes, and often in practice, the closing stock figure is usually taken.

Rate of finished stock turnover

This ratio tells us how many times the stock of finished goods is 'turned over' in the course of a year. We calculate it by taking either:

$$\frac{\text{Cost of sales sold}}{\text{Average finished goods stock}} = \text{No. of times stock is turned over in the year}$$

or:

$$\frac{\text{Average finished goods stock}}{\text{Cost of sales sold}} \times 365 = \text{No. of days' sales held in stock}$$

Figures for Auburn Ltd are:

$$\frac{6,000}{800} = 7.5 \text{ times} \quad and \quad \frac{800}{6,000} \times 365 = 49 \text{ days}$$

The level of stock required to support a given level of sales will vary from business to business.

As well as providing a means of appraising the efficiency of management in controlling stock, the ratio may be used to estimate the increase in stock necessary to support a budgeted increase in sales.

Raw materials stockholding and work-in-progress levels

There are two subsidiary stock ratios telling us how efficiently a company controls its raw materials stock and its work in progress:

$$\frac{\text{Raw materials stock}}{\text{Materials consumed}} \times 365$$

$$\frac{\text{Work-in-progress}}{\text{Cost of sales}} \times 365$$

For Auburn Ltd the figures are:

$$\frac{1{,}000}{3{,}500} \times 365 = 104 \text{ days} \quad \textit{and} \quad \frac{400}{6{,}000} \times 365 = 24 \text{ days}$$

Only experience in the industry concerned can tell us whether these are reasonable levels. Comparison with previous years can show whether the position is improving or deteriorating.

Debtors collection period

$$\frac{\text{Trade debtors}}{\text{Credit sales}} \times 365 = \text{No. of days' sales in debtors}$$

The figure for Auburn Ltd is:

$$\frac{1{,}300}{9{,}000} \times 365 = 53 \text{ days}$$

A reasonable average figure, for a business offering monthly credit terms, is 60 days. Note that it is important to eliminate non-trade debtors from the debtors total. (In examination questions an analysis of debtors is rarely provided, and the total debtors figure will therefore often have to be used.)

Creditors payment period

$$\frac{\text{Trade creditors}}{\text{Credit purchases}} \times 365 = \text{No. of days' purchases in creditors}$$

We do not know the purchases figure for Auburn Ltd and cannot be sure of the exact trade creditors, but a reasonable approximation can be obtained by using the figure of raw materials consumed (purchases adjusted for opening and closing stocks).

On this basis the figure for Auburn Ltd is:

$$\frac{1{,}150^*}{3{,}000} \times 365 = 140 \text{ days} \quad \text{(rather slow!)}$$

*The 1,150 is 1,800 minus 650 for tax and dividend.

As with debtors, 60 days is a reasonable average figure.

Fixed asset turnover

This ratio tells us the degree of fixed asset utilisation in generating turnover. The higher the ratio, the more effectively the fixed assets are being deployed, though of course the turnover ratios possible vary greatly from industry to industry.

The ratio is calculated as:

$$\frac{\text{Sales}}{\text{Average net book value of fixed assets}} : 1$$

For Auburn Ltd we have:

$$\frac{9{,}000}{3{,}000} : 1 = 3:1$$

It is preferable to use the *average* fixed assets for the calculation, but this information is often not available in examination questions.

A warning note is that this ratio can give a misleading view if asset values are based on depreciated historical cost without revaluation. In that case assets appear at below their true value, thus overstating the ratio and making the operation appear more efficient than it really is.

Working capital to turnover ratio

This tells us how effectively working capital (current assets minus current liabilities) is being deployed. The calculation is:

$$\frac{\text{Sales}}{\text{Working capital}} : 1$$

For Auburn Ltd the ratio is:

$$\frac{9,000}{2,000} : 1 = 4.5:1$$

Total asset turnover

This ratio is similar in purpose to the two previous ones, and tells us how effectively the *total* assets of the organisation are being utilised. The calculation is:

$$\frac{\text{Sales}}{\text{Total assets}} : 1$$

For Auburn Ltd we have:

$$\frac{9,000}{6,800} : 1 = 1.3:1$$

We may also use total assets less current liabilities in the calculation:

$$\frac{9,000}{5,000} = 1.8:1$$

It is a matter of taste which one is selected. The important point is, of course, to maintain comparability by consistent use of one or the other.

3.4 Gearing

One very important area we have not yet looked at is *gearing* (referred to in American books as 'leverage'). Gearing ratios measure the extent to which a company's operations are financed by loan capital, preference shares and possibly short-term borrowings as opposed to equity capital. There are several ways of expressing gearing:

(a) The debt/equity ratio:

$$\frac{\text{Fixed interest capital}}{\text{Equity share capital plus reserves}}$$

For Auburn Ltd we have:

$$\frac{2,000}{3,000} = 0.67$$

(b) Percentage of total capital provided by loan capital; i.e., for Auburn:

$$\frac{2,000}{5,000} \times 100 = 40\%$$

We may also express gearing in terms of the cost of different elements in the capital structure:

$$\frac{\text{Interest charges}}{\text{Profit before interest and dividends}}$$

$$\frac{240,000}{1,140,000} = 21\%$$

This tells us that 21% of the profit is absorbed by interest charges. If there were preference shares, the dividend on these would also have to be allowed for.

What are the implications of gearing? A highly geared company (one with a large proportion of its total capital provided by loans or debentures, etc.) is more vulnerable to a down-turn in profits, because the interest charges must be paid regardless of profit. Conversely, when profits are high, the equity shareholders benefit disproportionately, because the interest charges remain fixed despite the high profits.

Consider the following example:

	P Ltd £000	Q Ltd £000
Ordinary shares plus reserves	100	20
10% debentures	—	80
	100	100

Both companies have a total capital employed of £100,000. Let us see what happens at varying profit levels (taxation has been ignored to clarify the principle at work):

(a) Profit level £10,000: the shareholders of P Ltd have a yield of 10% on their investment. *So do the shareholders of Q Ltd*, because £8,000 of the £10,000 is taken up by debenture interest, leaving £2,000, or 10%, for the equity interest.

(b) Profit level £20,000: the shareholders of P Ltd have a yield of 20% on their investment. The shareholders of Q Ltd enjoy 60% — the debenture interest again takes £8,000 leaving £12,000, or 60% of £20,000 for equity.

(c) Profit level £5,000: the shareholders of P Ltd have a yield of 5%, but the shareholders in Q Ltd have a loss of £3,000 after paying the loan interest £8,000.

We can thus see that high gearing increases the risk for equity shareholders and, of course, for prospective lenders or granters of credit. Putting the results another way, we can say that the equity shareholders *gain* when the return on investment is greater than the interest percentage to be paid on loans, and *lose* when the return on investment is less than the interest rate.

3.5 Measures of return for investors

In the ratio for net profit as a percentage of capital employed we considered the return on capital employed, which we defined in various ways, usually including loan capital. The ordinary sharholders are interested in the return obtained by the use of their funds. To measure this we may use two ratios, one based on dividend and the other on earnings.

Dividend yield

The *dividend yield* is calculated by taking the *gross equivalent* of the dividend (which is paid net of income tax) as a percentage of the *market price* of the share. We take the gross equivalent so that we get a percentage comparable with percentage returns on other types of investment. Taking 30% as the basic rate of income tax, we gross up the dividend by multiplying by 10/7.

Earnings yield

The *earnings yield* is calculated by expressing 'earnings' as a percentage of the market price of the share, taking 'earnings' to mean earnings *after interest and tax* but *before* extraordinary items, if any.

The formulas are therefore:

$$\frac{\text{Grossed dividend per share}}{\text{Market price per share}} \times 100 = \text{Dividend yield}$$

$$\frac{\text{Earnings per share after tax and preference dividend}}{\text{Market price per share}} \times 100 = \text{Earnings yield}$$

For Auburn Ltd, assuming a market price per share of £2 or 200p, we have:

$$\text{Dividend yield} = \frac{10p^* \times 10/7}{200} \times 100 = 7.14\%$$

*Dividend of £200,000 paid on nominal capital of 2,000,000 £1 shares = 10p per share.

$$\text{Earnings yield} = \frac{29.25p^*}{200} \times 100 = 14.625\%$$

*Earnings of £585,000 related to nominal capital of 2,000,000 £1 shares = 29.25p per share.

Note

In the above ratios involving earnings, we should normally use the so-called *net basis* in calculating earnings, as indicated in SSAP 3. If, exceptionally, the *nil basis* was significantly different, a case could be made for calculating earnings per share on both bases.

Net basis: Earnings after deducting all elements in the taxation charge (i.e., as in profit and loss account).
Nil basis: Earnings after deducting only tax arising if distributions had been nil (i.e., excluding irrecoverable ACT from the calculation).

The price/earnings ratio (P/E ratio)

You may have seen reference in the Financial Times share prices to the 'P/E ratio'. This is another way of expressing the relationships between earnings per share and price per share. The P/E ratio is:

$$\frac{\text{Price per share}}{\text{Earnings per share}}$$

For Auburn Ltd it is

$$\frac{200p}{29.25p} = 6.84$$

The earnings yield and P/E ratio are reciprocals of each other: 14.625% × 6.84 = 100%.

Dividend cover

The dividend cover is the number of times the ordinary dividend paid is covered by the earnings.

$$\frac{\text{Earnings after tax and preference dividend}}{\text{Ordinary dividend paid}} = \text{Dividend cover}$$

For Auburn Ltd we have:

$$\frac{585}{200} = 2.925 \text{ times}$$

The ratios in this subsection allow us to compare one company's performance as an investment with that of others, or to compare investment in a company with other types of investment. The dividend cover tells us what proportion of earnings a company normally pays out as dividend, and how easy it will be for the company to maintain the dividend should earnings fall.

3.6 Employment statistics

A company's financial statements provide information about employees which may be the basis of ratios offering interesting comparisons between companies:

(a) Average remuneration per employee:

$$\frac{\text{Total payroll}}{\text{Average number of employees}}$$

(b) Turnover per employee:

$$\frac{\text{Turnover}}{\text{Average number of employees}}$$

(c) Net profit per employee:

$$\frac{\text{Net profit before interest and tax}}{\text{Average number of employees}}$$

(d) Degree of mechanisation, or capital invested per employee:

$$\frac{\text{Fixed assets}}{\text{Average number of employees}}$$

or

$$\frac{\text{Cost of plant and machinery}}{\text{Average number of employees}}$$

4 REPORT WRITING

Many examination questions call for a 'report' based on ratio analysis of given information about a company or companies. Your answer must therefore consist of calculations of relevant ratios plus their interpretation, the whole answer being presented in the form of a report. What does the examiner mean by a 'report'? It is difficult to be quite sure. The notes which follow present some guidance as to what is likely to be expected.

Every report should consist of three basic parts:

(a) an *introduction,* in which the terms of reference are stated;
(b) the *main body* of the report, in which facts are presented;
(c) a statement of the *conclusions and recommendations* of the report.

In a question on interpretation, and indeed in many accounting questions, the report will be based on calculations that have to be made before the conclusions to be reached in the report can be arrived at. The sensible way to handle this, both in practice and in the examination, is to do all the calculations *first*, head them 'Appendix 1', then refer to them as you write the main body of the report.

Another problem is the heading and conclusion to the report. Here we should distinguish between internal and external reports. If the question asks you to report as chief accountant to the managing director, you are writing an internal report, and an appropriate form of heading could be:

To: Managing Director

From: Chief Accountant   Date:

Report on --------------------

The report would then deal with the three stages indicated above, with appendices as necessary.

If the question asks you to report as a professional accountant to a client, the report is an external one, and the form of heading will be:

```
                                              A B & Co
                                              High Street
                                              London
The Managing Director
X Limited
Birmingham
                                              Date
Dear Sir

Report on --------------------
```

The remainder of the report could then follow in exactly the same form as before, with a signature 'A B & Co' at the end.

5 A BASIC EXAMPLE

5.1 Question

Cee Ltd and Dee Ltd are subsidiaries of Eff plc. They are in the same trade but operate in different areas. Their accounts for the year ended 30 September 19X2 are as follows.

	Cee Ltd		Dee Ltd	
Profit and loss account	£000	£000	£000	£000
Sales		720		860
Less: Cost of sales		560		671
Gross profit		160		189
Less: Overheads		110		150
Net profit before tax		50		39
Corporation tax	20		15	
Dividend	10	30	12	27
Retained profit for the year		20		12
Balance sheet				
Share capital		300		100
Reserves		120		52
		420		152
8% debentures		—		60
		420		212

	Cee Ltd		Dee Ltd	
	£000	£000	£000	£000
Represented by:				
Fixed assets				
Cost		330		260
Less: Depreciation		100		80
		230		180
Current assets				
Stock	140		86	
Debtors	155		150	
Cash	15		16	
	310		252	
Less: Current liabilities				
Taxation	20		15	
Creditors	90		172	
Bank overdraft	—		21	
Dividend	10		12	
	120		220	
Net current assets		190		32
		420		212

All sales are on credit terms.

You are required to:

(a) Compare the profitability and the financial position of the two companies, using suitable ratios.

(b) Comment briefly on your findings.

5.2 Answer

(a) (i) Profitability   Cee Ltd   Dee Ltd

Return on capital employed
50/420 × 100   11.9%
(39 + 4.8*)/212 × 100   20.7%

*4.8 is the interest on the debentures:
£60,000 @ 8%

Return on shareholders' capital
30/420   7.1%
24/152   15.8%

Gross profit: Sales
160/720 × 100   22.2%
189/860 × 100   22.0%

Net profit: Sales
50/720 × 100   6.9%
39/860 × 100   4.5%

Turnover: Capital employed
720:420   1.7 times
860:212   4.1 times

(ii) Liquidity

Current assets/Current liabilities
310/120   2.6:1
252/220   1.1:1

Quick assets/Current liabilities
170/120   1.4:1
166/220   0.75:1

(iii) Management efficiency

Stock: Cost of sales
140/560 × 365   91 days
86/671 × 365   47 days

Debtors: Sales
155/720 × 365   79 days
150/860 × 365   64 days

Creditors: Purchases
(based on Creditors: Cost of sales)
90/560 × 365   59 days
172/671 × 365   94 days

(iv) Gearing

Fixed interest capital/Total capital
0/420   Nil
60/212   28%
Debt: Equity
60/152   39%
                                              (or 1:2.5)

(b) Comments

(i) Profitability

Dee Ltd shows a considerably better return on capital employed (20.7% against 11.9% for Cee Ltd). This is partly accounted for by the much higher use of trade creditors as finance by Dee (94 days credit taken against 59 days for Cee).

The difference in the return on shareholders' funds (15.8% against 7.1%) is even more marked, reflecting the beneficial effect of the gearing (28% in Dee against nil in Cee).

The gross profit margin is much the same for the two companies at about 22%. The net profit is lower for Dee, partly as a result of the interest on the debentures and bank overdraft. Dee Ltd compensates, however, by its much higher activity level evidenced by the ratio of turnover to capital employed (1.7 times for Cee, 4.1 times for Dee).

(ii) Liquidity

Cee Ltd has higher liquidity ratios than Dee. In fact, Cee's current ratio and quick ratio are too high at 2.6:1 and 1.4:1, indicating potential availability of funds now in current assets which could with advantage be redeployed in income-producing fixed assets. Dee Ltd, on the other hand, has very tight ratios and is in need of more working capital.

(iii) Management efficiency

Cee Ltd has nearly twice as many days' stock to support sales as Dee Ltd (91 days against 47 days.) The credit period allowed to customers is also higher at Cee (79 days against 64 days). These ratios could indicate some slackness of control over stock and debtors at Cee Ltd. As regards payment of creditors, however, Dee Ltd is not maintaining an acceptable standard, unless exceptionally long credit terms have been negotiated, perhaps with Eff Ltd, the holding company.

(iv) Gearing

Only Dee Ltd has any loan capital. Its 28% finance from debentures has contributed to the improved return it obtains on shareholders' funds, as explained in (b)(i) above.

6 A MORE ADVANCED EXAMPLE

6.1 Question

W plc is a listed company engaged in the fabrication and erection of modular steel structures.

The company's recent history of sales and profits is as follows:

Year ended 30 September:	19X2	19X3	19X4	19X5
Turnover: Home (£000)	4,771	3,221	4,077	3,707
Export (£000)	4,441	7,362	8,152	4,773
Profit before tax as percentage of sales	9.7%	9.7%	9.3%	4.4%
Earnings per share	18.4p	30.9p	30.0p	8.9p
Ordinary dividend per share	7.7p	8.1p	9.1p	9.1p

Following publication of the 19X5 annual report, a worried shareholder has asked for your independent comments on the financial management of the business during 19X5.

The information you consider most relevant is reproduced in the following appendices to this question:

Appendix A	Your own version of the 19X5 Source and Application of Funds Statement.
Appendix B	Abbreviated balance sheets as at 30 September 19X4 and 19X5.
Appendix C	Miscellaneous extracts from the annual report.

You are required to set out your preliminary views (subject to further enquiry) on the financial management of the company during the year 19X4/X5, using the information provided and making any calculations you consider relevant.

Appendix A

W plc Source and application of funds statement for year ended 30 September 19X5

	£000	£000
Profit before interest and taxation		380
Add: Items not involving the movement of funds:		
depreciation	521	
other	4	
		525
		905
Reduction in working capital (stocks, debtors and creditors)		1,109
Operating cash flow		2,014
Fixed assets:		
purchases	(921)	
sales	25	
		(896)
Cash payment on acquisition of new subsidiary (see note below)		(1,425)
		(307)
Tax paid		(143)
		(450)
Reduction in liquid assets		361
Entity cash flow (out)		(89)

	£000	£000
Equity cash flow:		
Dividends paid	(283)	
Shares issued	43	
		(240)
Lender cash flow:		
Interest paid	(7)	
Bank overdraft obtained	336	
		329
		89

Note: On 27 September 19X5 the company diversified its activities by the acquisition of the whole share capital of S Ltd. The total acquisition price was £3,658,000, satisfied by:

	£000	
Cash	1,425	
New ordinary shares	67	⎫ Not shown in
Unsecured borrowing	2,166	⎬ the Source
	3,658	⎭ and Application of Funds Statement

		£000
The net assets acquired were:		
Tangible fixed assets		624
Stocks		556
Trade debtors		669
Cash at bank		679
		2,528
Trade creditors	379	
Other liabilities	279	
		658
		1,870
Goodwill		1,788
		3,658

Goodwill has been written off against reserves.

W plc profit and loss account for the year ended 30 September 19X5 does not include any figures relating to S Ltd.

Appendix B

W plc Consolidated balance sheet at 30 September 19X5

	19X5		19X4	
	£000	£000	£000	£000
Fixed assets:				
Tangible fixed assets		4,283		3,290
Investments		1,437		1,399
		5,720		4,689
Current assets:				
Stocks and work-in-progress	3,141		2,792	
Trade debtors	2,289		2,654	
Other debtors	280		396	
Cash at bank and in hand	792		522	
	6,502		6,364	
Creditors — amounts falling due within one year:				
Bank overdraft	336		—	
Trade creditors	1,382		806	
Other creditors	1,387		1,513	
	3,105		2,319	
Net current assets		3,397		4,045
Total assets less current liabilities (carried forward)		9,117		8,734

	19X5	19X4
	£000	£000
Brought forward	9,117	8,734
Creditors — amounts falling due after more than one year:		
Unsecured loan	(2,166)	—
Deferred taxation	(593)	(229)
Net assets	6,358	8,505
Capital and reserves:		
Called-up share capital	3,287	3,177
Revaluation reserve	487	449
Profit and loss account	2,584	4,879
	6,358	8,505

Appendix C

W plc Miscellaneous extracts from the annual report for the year ended 30 September 19X5

1 Tangible fixed assets

	Land and buildings	Plant and machinery	Total
	£000	£000	£000
Cost:			
At 30 September 19X4	2,212	2,400	4,612
Additions	285	635	920
Subsidiary acquired	555	109	664
Disposals	(34)	(160)	(194)
At 30 September 19X5	3,018	2,984	6,002
Depreciation provision:			
At 30 September 19X4	284	1,038	1,322
Provisions for year	227	294	521
Subsidiary acquired	—	40	40
Disposals	(34)	(130)	(164)
At 30 September 19X5	477	1,242	1,719

	Land and buildings £000	Plant and machinery £000	Total £000
Net book value:			
At 30 September 19X4	1,928	1,362	3,290
At 30 September 19X5	2,541	1,742	4,283

2 Stocks and work-in-progress

		19X5 £000		19X4 £000
Raw materials		635		682
Finished goods		1,950		1,680
Contract work-in-progress	847		440	
Less: progress payments received	291		10	
		556		430
		3,141		2,792

3 Profit and loss account balance

	£000	£000	£000
Balance at 30 September 19X4			4,879
Profit for year ended 30 September 19X5:			
Before interest and tax		380	
Less:			
Interest	7		
Tax	95		
Extraordinary item — provision for deferred taxation	496		
Dividends	289		
		887	
			(507)
			4,372
Goodwill written off — acquisition of subsidiary			1,788
Balance at 30 September 19X5			2,584

4   Employees

	19X5	19X4
Average weekly number of employees:		
Manufacture	244	248
Selling	49	46
Administration	127	131
	420	425
Average remuneration per employee	£7,525	£7,300

6.2 Discussion

An interesting question from which several things can be learnt (it comes from the ICMA Financial Management paper of November 1985). Before we begin to tackle the answer, let us study the very useful format of the funds statement in Appendix A. The use of a slightly different format highlights some useful information. First of all, note the way that the net movement in working capital is added to the funds generated from operations to give a sub-heading of *operating cash flow* — resources available to finance purchase of fixed assets and out of which tax and dividends are paid. After fixed asset acquisitions and tax are deducted, and the reduction of liquid assets accounted for, we have *entity cash flow*. This is then analysed into *equity cash flow* and *lender cash flow*. Not, perhaps, a format to adopt in examination questions on funds flow statements because of the additional time required, but nonetheless an interesting and informative method of presentation.

Returning to the approach to answering the question, we must first of all identify the important events for the year.

The shareholder is clearly 'worried' because profits have fallen sharply, and the dividend is not covered by earnings. Possible causes are the sharp decline in export sales, and the smaller but still perceptible decline in home sales.

The position is partially obscured by the fact that the balance sheet includes the assets and liabilities of S Ltd. If we are to calculate meaningful ratios, the balance sheet items will require adjustment to eliminate these.

The question asks for 'preliminary views' and hence presumably does not require a report format. The answer should include plenty of references to further information needed. On the basis of the data presented in the question it is impossible to reach firm conclusions; only tentative explanations can be advanced for many matters.

6.3 Answer

Preliminary views on the financial management of W plc, year ended 30 September 19X5

Working capital management

The net working capital of W plc has gone down by £1.1 million. The acquisition of S Ltd required the expenditure of £1,425,000 cash but led to the addition of £1,246,000 to the working capital in the W plc consolidated balance sheet. The £1.1 million reduction thus largely reflects other action by the W plc management. The working capital reduction is mainly the result of increases in creditors.

The ratios and comments in Appendix A throw some light on the movements which have taken place in individual elements of working capital.

The debtors payment period has improved from 79.2 days to 69.7 days. This could reflect the fact that a smaller proportion of sales, and hence presumably of debtors, is attributable to export sales, since export sales might have involved the granting of longer credit terms. This aspect of the working capital management appears satisfactory.

The creditors payment period has been extended to a considerable extent. Such a policy cannot be acceptable on a long-term basis as it will damage the company's credit status. Efficient future management of the combined resources of W plc and S Ltd should render such a policy unnecessary, provided profits are adequate.

Stocks, ignoring those of S Ltd, have not fallen as much as might have been expected in view of the decline in turnover.

The current ratio and liquid ratio both show an acceptable position at 30 September 19X5. The nature of the business probably means that the current ratio must be rather high because of the necessarily high stocks. Comparison with other similar businesses could be enlightening.

Overall, working capital management appears to have been less than perfect, possibly because the company has had to contend with sharply declining sales and with the need to accumulate a substantial cash balance to finance the acquisition of S Ltd.

Loan capital
The company has borrowed £2,166,000 towards financing the purchase of S Ltd. This, together with the bank overdraft of £336,000, implies an interest charge of perhaps £300,000 (12% of £2.5m), and possibly more. Such a heavy interest burden could place a considerable strain on the company in future years. The profit forecasts of W plc and S Ltd would be interesting. One might check to see if any indication of future prospects appeared in the chairman's statement accompanying the published financial statements of W plc.

The fact that the company has succeeded in obtaining an unsecured loan of such an amount indicates that the lender appears to have faith in the company's ability to recover from the poor results of 19X4/X5.

Acquisition of S Ltd
The acquisition of S Ltd could place strain on the financial management of the group in 19X5/X6. The nature of the business conducted by S Ltd is not indicated. The high value placed on the goodwill suggests that it will make a contribution to the group in excess of the interest charge on the unsecured loan.

Sundry matters
There are a number of matters on which further information would be useful to amplify the views expressed above. These include:

(a) the reason for the decline in sales and especially export sales;
(b) profit forecasts of W plc and S Ltd;

(c) the reason for the substantial provision for deferred taxation;
(d) the reason why there was no material reduction in the workforce in the face of sharply decreased turnover and profit.

Conclusion

The year ended 30 September 19X5 was a difficult one for the management of W plc. The reduced profit, converted to a loss after tax and extraordinary items, and the reduced turnover are symptoms of a rapid decline in the company's fortunes. The company must restore its position in the year ending 30 September 19X6, and ensure that S Ltd justifies the substantial amount paid for its goodwill. Management has indicated its confidence in the future by maintaining the dividend in a year when the company has made a loss, and the unsecured lenders and the bank have demonstrated their faith in the company by respectively making a loan and granting an overdraft, the latter providing funds for the 19X5 dividend. The shareholder should probably hold on to his shares for the time being but watch the company's progress closely.

Appendix A Ratios and comments concerning working capital items

Debtors payment period

19X5: $(2,289 - 669)/8,480 \times 365 = 69.7$ days
19X4: $2,654/12,229 \times 365 = 79.2$ days

Creditors payment period

We have insufficient data to calculate this ratio. Trade creditors have, however, increased from £806,000 at 30 September 19X4 to £1,002,000 at 30 September 19X5, excluding the trade creditors of S Ltd. As sales have fallen sharply, it is likely that considerably extended credit has been taken from suppliers.

Stocks

It is not clear where the £556,000 stock of S Ltd appears in the stock and work-in-progress total of £3,141,000. Excluding S Ltd, total stock has gone down, though not by as much as the fall in sales might be expected to cause.

The comparable rates of total stock turnover are:

19X5: 8,480/2,585 = 3.3 times
19X4: 12,229/2,792 = 4.4 times

A significant deterioration.

The apparent increase in the finished goods stock may be because of the inclusion of part of the £556,000 stock of S Ltd under this heading.

Current ratio

19X5: 6,502/3,105 = 2.1:1
19X5   ignoring acquisition of S Ltd:

$$\frac{6,502 - 1,904 + 1,425}{3,105 - 658} = \frac{6,023}{2,447} = 2.5:1$$

19X4: 6,364/2,319 = 2.7:1

Quick ratio

19X5: 3,361/3,105 = 1.1:1
19X4: 3,572/2,319 = 1.5:1

7 TEST QUESTION AND ANSWER

7.1 Question

P Ltd has traded profitably for many years and, since moving to a new factory in 1970, its turnover has risen annually.

From the information given below, you are required to prepare a report for the board of directors of P Ltd assessing the performance of P Ltd from 19X1 to 19X5, including an analysis of its profitability and financial position.

Abstracts from the financial statements of P Ltd for the five years ended 31 December 19X5 are set out below:

Profit and loss accounts

	19X1 £	19X2 £	19X3 £	19X4 £	19X5 £
Turnover	4,500,000	4,980,000	5,994,000	6,720,000	8,100,000
Purchases	3,781,200	4,188,000	5,152,800	5,734,200	7,101,000
Increase in stocks	33,000	64,200	204,000	168,600	305,400
	3,748,200	4,123,800	4,948,800	5,565,600	6,795,600
Gross profit	751,800	856,200	1,045,200	1,154,400	1,304,400
Staff costs	411,400	461,200	551,000	599,800	668,600
Depreciation	43,200	45,600	45,000	46,200	45,600
Other operating charges	104,000	117,800	146,200	155,000	176,200
	558,600	624,600	742,200	801,000	890,400
Operating profit	193,200	231,600	303,000	353,400	414,000
Bank interest	—	7,200	14,400	34,800	51,600
Profit before taxation	193,200	224,400	288,600	318,600	362,400
Taxation	110,400	114,600	121,800	142,500	157,200
Profit after taxation	82,800	109,800	166,800	176,100	205,200
Retained profits brought forward	188,400	200,700	240,000	334,800	438,900
	271,200	310,500	406,800	510,900	644,100
Dividend	70,500	70,500	72,000	72,000	72,000
Retained profits carried forward	200,700	240,000	334,800	438,900	572,100

Balance sheets as at 31 December

	19X1 £	19X2 £	19X3 £	19X4 £	19X5 £
Fixed assets:					
Land and buildings at cost	1,080,000	1,080,000	1,080,000	1,080,000	1,080,000
Machinery at cost less depreciation	354,000	367,800	360,000	369,000	366,000
	1,434,000	1,447,800	1,440,000	1,449,000	1,446,000
Current assets:					
Stocks	612,000	676,200	880,200	1,048,800	1,354,200
Debtors	379,200	433,500	514,800	619,500	739,500
Cash	6,600	5,400	3,600	3,900	2,700
	997,800	1,115,100	1,398,600	1,672,200	2,096,400
Creditors: amounts falling due within one year:					
Trade creditors	310,200	330,600	406,200	411,000	468,900
Taxation and dividend payable	180,900	185,100	193,800	214,500	229,200
Bank overdraft	—	67,200	163,800	316,800	532,200
	491,100	582,900	763,800	942,300	1,230,300
Net current assets	506,700	532,200	634,800	729,900	866,100
Total assets less current liabilities	1,940,700	1,980,000	2,074,800	2,178,900	2,312,100
Capital and reserves:					
Ordinary share capital	1,500,000	1,500,000	1,500,000	1,500,000	1,500,000
Capital reserve	240,000	240,000	240,000	240,000	240,000
Retained profits	200,700	240,000	334,800	438,900	572,100
	1,940,700	1,980,000	2,074,800	2,178,900	2,312,100

Note: The selling price index of the goods sold by P Ltd is as follows:

19X1	19X2	19X3	19X4	19X5
100	120	150	180	200

7.2 Discussion

The question asks for a *report*. That means a report format, and an appendix in which the ratios and percentages supporting your conclusions are detailed.

The selling price index figures at the end of the question invite the calculation of inflation-adjusted sales figures to check the rate of real growth over the years to be considered.

The two main areas to be considered are profitability and 'financial position'. This second requirement immediately suggests liquidity, amplified by the ratios for stock turnover and debtors and creditors payment periods.

It is clear from the balance sheet that land and buildings have not been depreciated (in relation to buildings this is in contravention of SSAP 12 and the Companies Act!), and that they have not been revalued, implying that fixed asset values are almost certainly understated. Return on capital employed is thus progressively overstated.

There are no debentures or loans. This reduces the risk of calculating an unsound percentage of return on capital employed, but note the substantial and increasing bank overdraft, which should probably be treated as long-term capital for the purpose of analysis.

Figures for five years are given. It is probably best, for examination purposes, to concentrate on calculations for the first year and the last, investigating the intermediate years only if time permits. We should consider preparing statements of source and application of funds for the years involved also. Even when not specifically asked for, it is a good idea to prepare these in answering an interpretation question, and then, of course, say something intelligent about what they show! A statement has not been prepared as part of the suggested answer to this question, because it was thought that time did not realistically allow for this. A tutorial note following the suggested answer presents such a statement with brief comments.

7.3 Answer

To: The Board of Directors of P Ltd
From: Chief Accountant

14 March 19X6

Report on the profitability and financial position of P Ltd, 19X1 to 19X5

As requested in your memorandum dated 28 February 19X6, I have made an analysis of the company's profitability and financial position over the five years to 31 December 19X5.

My conclusions and recommendations are presented below. Details of the ratios used and their calculation are in Appendix 1. References after each ratio are to their number in this Appendix.

Profitability

Using the figures in the balance sheets without adjustment, the return on capital employed appears to have improved from 10% in 19X1 to 14.6% in 19X5 (ratio 1). This increase is more apparent than real, however, as the land and buildings making up approximately three-quarters of the capital employed have not been revalued during this period and are most probably considerably undervalued as a result. If asset values were adjusted to current values there would probably be a decline in the percentage of return earned.

The improvement in the post-tax return on shareholders' funds, from 4.3% to 8.9% (ratio 2), would also be much eroded by a revaluation of assets.

Gross profit as a percentage of sales has declined slightly over the period, from 16.7% in 19X1 to 16.1% in 19X5 (ratio 3). Other operating costs have remained fairly constant at 2.2%-2.3% (ratio 5), while wages costs have fallen slightly from 9% to 8.3% (ratio 4). At the net level the profit percentage before bank interest has risen from 4.3% to 5.1% (ratio 6). It is difficult to draw any firm conclusions from the rather small movements in this group of percentages.

Reference was made above to the effect of inflation on the percentage return on capital employed. The apparent growth in turnover and profits over the period (from a turnover of £4.5m in 19X1 to £8.1m in 19X5 and profits before taxation rising from £193,200 to £362,400) should be seen against the background of inflation rates applicable to the goods sold which have effectively halved their value. When the sales are adjusted for inflation (ratio 7) it can be seen that sales declined by 17% in volume over the period 19X1 to 19X4, recovering by 8% in 19X5, but nevertheless showing an overall decline from 19X1 to 19X5 of 10%. Profit before tax from 19X1 to 19X5 adjusted in the same way declined by 6%.

Liquidity

The company's liquid position has declined over the years, but is still at an overall level giving no real cause for concern. The company is increasingly relying on a bank overdraft, however, and if this liability is regarded as a quick liability the ratio of quick assets to current liabilities (ratio 10) shows a decline to a level of 0.6:1 which could indicate potential future liquidity problems. If the overdraft is regarded as a longer-term source of funds in practical terms the ratio returns to a more acceptable level at 1.1:1 (ratio 11).

The levels of some of the ratios dealing with individual components of the working capital give cause for concern, and suggestions for action are set out below:

(a) Stock turnover ratio (ratio 12): the number of days' sales held in stock has risen from 60 days in 19X1 to 73 days in 19X5. If the company had managed to retain the stock level of 19X1, the stock figure would have been £237,000 less.

(b) Number of days' sales in debtors (ratio 13): the ratio has declined very slightly from 31 days to 33 days, a very satisfactory figure reflecting consistently good credit control.

(c) Number of days' purchases in creditors (ratio 14): the 30-day level of 19X1 indicated very prompt settlement, and this has tightened to the surprisingly low level of 24 days in 19X5. This could be the result of very prompt payment to major suppliers to obtain a cash discount, perhaps for payment within seven days. If the company could revert to the 30-day period of 19X1 without penalty the creditors would rise by about £115,000. If an increase to 45 days, a perfectly normal period, could be achieved, the creditors would rise by over £400,000 and this, combined with the economies on stockholding suggested in (a) would completely eliminate the bank overdraft, leading to a cash balance of some £110,000 and the saving of the interest charge currently running at over £50,000 per year.

Conclusions

The overall picture presented by the analysis above is of declining real turnover combined with deteriorating liquidity. Increases in stocks and reductions in creditors have led to a bank overdraft of over £500,000. The possibility of restricting the working capital along the lines indicated should be urgently investigated. The company's long-term future, however, depends on improvement in volume of sales — a process begun in 19X4/X5, which must continue.

Expenditure on new plant has been limited over the period investigated, being very little more than the annual depreciation charge. It may well be that further investment in plant is necessary to revitalise the company, financed by a rights issue of ordinary shares or by loan capital secured on the land and buildings.

One good feature which could facilitate the raising of fresh capital is that earnings are considerably in excess of the dividend, which has not been increased since 19X3, and then only by a modest amount, while cover has risen from 1.2% in 19X1 to 2.9% in 19X5.

Appendix 1   Ratios

Profitability		19X1	19X5
1	Return on capital employed		
	$193,200/1,940,700 \times 100$	10.0%	
	$414,000/(2,312,100 + 532,200) \times 100$		14.6%
2	Return on shareholders' funds		
	$82,800/1,940,700 \times 100$	4.3%	
	$205,200/2,312,100 \times 100$		8.9%

			19X1	19X5

3   Gross profit on sales
       751,800/4,500,000   16.7%
       1,304,400/8,100,000   16.1%

4   Wages costs as percentage of sales
       411,400/4,500,000 × 100   9.1%
       668,600/8,100,000 × 100   8.3%

5   Other operating costs as percentage of sales
       104,000/4,500,000 × 100   2.3%
       176,200/8,100,000 × 100   2.2%

6   Operating profit as percentage of sales
       193,200/4,500,000 × 100   4.3%
       414,000/8,100,000 × 100   5.1%

7   Turnover adjusted for movement in selling price index:

	£	
19X1	4,500,000	19X1-X4: down 17%
19X2	4,150,000	19X4-X5: up 8%
19X3	3,996,000	19X1-X5: down 10%
19X4	3,733,333	
19X5	4,050,000	

8   Profit before taxation adjusted for movement in selling price index:

	£
19X1	193,200
19X5	181,200: down 6%

Liquidity   19X1   19X5

9   Current assets/current liabilities
       997,800/491,100   2.0:1
       2,096,400/1,230,300   1.7:1

10   Quick assets/current liabilities
       385,800/491,100   0.8:1
       742,200/1,230,300   0.6:1

		19X1	19X5
11	Quick assets/quick liabilities (excluding bank overdraft)		
	385,800/491,100	0.8:1	
	742,200/698,100		1.1:1
12	Stock turnover ratio		
	612,000/3,748,200 × 365	60 days	
	1,354,200/6,795,600 × 365		73 days
13	Debtors to sales		
	379,200/4,500,000 × 365	31 days	
	739,500/8,100,000 × 365		33 days
14	Creditors to purchases		
	310,200/3,781,200 × 365	30 days	
	468,900/7,101,000 × 365		24 days

Tutorial note

The funds flow statements shown below are for illustrative purposes.

	19X2 £000	19X3 £000	19X4 £000	19X5 £000
Sources:				
Net profit before taxation	224.4	288.6	318.6	362.4
Add: Depreciation	45.6	45.0	46.2	45.6
Funds generated from operations	270.0	333.6	364.8	408.0
Applications:				
Purchases of machinery (net of sales)	(59.4)	(37.2)	(55.2)	(42.6)
Tax paid	(110.4)	(114.6)	(121.8)	(142.5)
Dividends paid	(70.5)	(70.5)	(72.0)	(72.0)
	29.7	111.3	115.8	150.9

	19X2 £000	19X3 £000	19X4 £000	19X5 £000
Net movements in working capital:				
Increase in stocks	64.2	204.0	168.6	305.4
Increase in debtors	54.3	81.3	104.7	120.0
Increase/(Decrease) in cash	(1.2)	(1.8)	0.3	(1.2)
Increase in trade creditors	(20.4)	(75.6)	(4.8)	(57.9)
Increase in bank overdraft	(67.2)	(96.6)	(153.0)	(215.4)
	29.7	111.3	115.8	150.9

The statements show clearly the extent to which the company's capital has been increasingly deployed in current assets rather than in purchase of new fixed assets. The steady growth in bank overdraft to finance the considerable increases in debtors and particularly in stock are also shown.